What Can You with a Ball of String?

By Stephen Gard
Illustrated by Bettina Guthridge

Shannon went to stay with Nanna. Shannon and Nanna went shopping.

"Will you buy me that, Nanna?" asked Shannon.

"No," said Nanna. "You will soon get tired of it."

Nanna pointed to something on a shelf. "There," she said. "I'll buy you one of those."

"A ball of string?" said Shannon. "What can you do with a ball of string?"

"I'll show you," said Nanna.

On Sunday, Nanna and Shannon took cardboard, paint, paste, and the ball of string into the kitchen. Soon, a puppet was dancing on the table.

On Monday, they took hooks, bait, a bucket, and the ball of string to the creek.

Soon, a fish was dangling from the string.

On Tuesday, they took sticks, paper, tape, and the ball of string to the park.

Soon, two kites climbed into the sky.

On Wednesday, they took spades, seeds, and the ball of string into the garden.

"Soon, beans will be climbing up," said Nanna.

On Thursday, they took a basket, a pulley, and the ball of string out to a tree in the garden.
Soon, Teddy was whizzing through the air!

On Friday, they each took a tin can and tied them to the string.

"Come inside for lunch now, please!" said Nanna.

On Saturday, Shannon went back home. She ran next door to see Rosa.

"Look what Nanna gave me!" she said. "A ball of string!"

"A ball of string?" said Rosa. "What can you do with a ball of string?"

"I'll show you," said Shannon.